If you don't know where you're going, you'll probably end up somewhere else

David Campbell, Ph.D.

TABOR®

PUBLISHING

Allen, Texas

CONTENTS

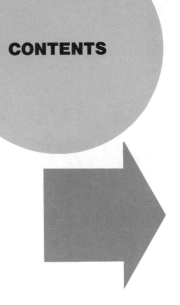

Cover design by Gene Tarpey
Book illustrations by Nicole Hollander

Send all inquiries to:
Tabor Publishing
One DLM Park
Allen, Texas 75002

Library of Congress Catalog Card Number 74-84711

Printed in the United States of America

ISBN 1-55924-373-2

2 3 4 5   94 93 92 91

PREFACE

You have to take life as it happens,
but you should try
to make it happen
the way you want to take it.

An old German saying

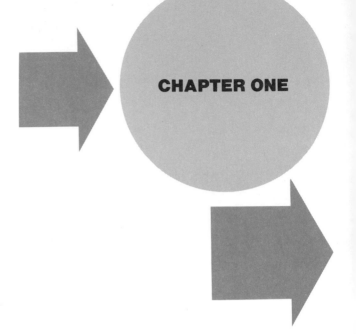

CHAPTER ONE

"Cheshire-Puss," . . . said Alice, "would you tell me, please, which way I ought to go from here?"

"That depends a good deal on where you want to get to," said the Cat.

"I don't much care where—" said Alice.

"Then it doesn't matter which way you go," said the Cat.

"—so long as I get somewhere," Alice added as an explanation.

"Oh, you're sure to do that," said the Cat, "if you only walk long enough."

Lewis Carroll, *Alice's Adventures in Wonderland*

The Road to Somewhere

Unless you know what you want from life, you are not likely to stumble across it. How do you know what you want? Especially if you are in some "the-future-is-misty" stage and are not quite certain where you are heading, how do you decide what will be important in your future?

From my interviews with hundreds of people about their hopes and plans, and from my surveys of thousands of people about their careers, I have learned that what most people want out of life, more than anything else, is the opportunity to make choices. The worst possible life is a life without choices, a life barren of the hope of new things, a life of blind alleys. In contrast, the most pleasant life is the life with the most opportunities.

For example, here are several possible outcomes of life. Which of them appeal to you?

1 Having an interesting job.

2 Having a good marriage.

3 Running your own company (or your own laboratory, or your own ranch, or your own office).

4 Living overseas in a beautiful village by the sea.

5 Spending time with interesting friends.

6 Having a comfortable home in the suburbs.

7 Living in a modern apartment resort in the heart of an exciting city.

8 Having enough free time and money to travel.

9 Producing a great work of art, or making an important scientific discovery, or devising a better master plan for a city, or making a run-down farm profitable.

10 Getting to know your family.

11 Staying in good physical condition.

12 Having people come to you because you are an expert.

13 Making enough money to travel, educate your children, and buy good art.

14 Working in an important government post, influencing what is happening in our country.

If you are like most people, many of these appeal to you. You might even answer, "I'd like to have almost all of those things happen to me at one time or another." What you are saying is that you want to have as many opportunities as possible so that you can pick and choose.

This is what this book is all about—creating opportunities for yourself. Sooner or later, you will realize that the greatest tragedy in life is to have no options, to have no choices. Consequently, when you are planning your future, you should plan it in a way that will give you some choices, and this approach is particularly important if you aren't really sure right now what you want to do. Some people when they are uncertain have a tendency to do nothing, and this substantially restricts their future choices. Even if you don't know what you want to do in the long run, you can do some things in the short run that will give you more choices when the long run gets here.

Some people
when they are uncertain
have a tendency to do nothing.

What do you do to make certain you will have future choices? To begin with, you can set some goals for yourself so you won't drift aimlessly, *but* they have to be the right kind of goals. The average person, when asked what he or she wants from life, replies with fairly specific goals, such as "a good education, a good job, a good marriage, a family, a pleasant home, travel, money, success."

For two reasons, such aims are not very useful in helping you plan a satisfying life. First, these goals are fixed, unchanging, while life is just the opposite, dynamic, fluctuating, always changing. To say, for example, that you want a good job implies that there is a job somewhere that will keep you happy indefinitely. Or to yearn for a good marriage implies that once you find the right person to marry, you will live happily ever after.

Well, it isn't that way. Practically all goals tarnish with time if not renewed in some way. A job that is exhilarating during the first year becomes less so after five years; without renewal, it becomes an automatic activity after ten years, and a prison after twenty. The same for a marriage. The divorce rate, perhaps the best indication of marriage failure, continues to climb and demonstrates that even relationships of love ("till death do us part") can weaken and change with time if there are no changes.

The second reason that such specific goals are not the best focus for our strivings is that,

Practically all goals
tarnish with time
if not renewed in some way.

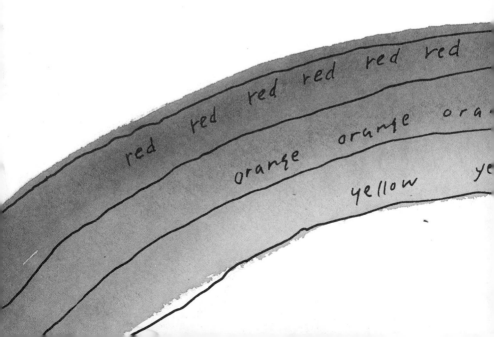

red

orange

yellow

yellow

yellow

once attained, they no longer seem so important. To be promoted, to make $25,000, to marry the most important person in the world, to win the Gold Medal, to earn the degree, to reach the quota—these are the carrots that we strive for, and they are pleasant at first, extraordinarily so, but without continual growth they pale. Emily Dickinson wrote, "Success is counted sweetest by those who ne'er succeed"; 'Adam Smith' said it in *The Money Game,* a fascinating book on what motivates people to play the stock market: "No specific goal can sustain one for very long after it is achieved."

Goals are useful, to be sure—much of this book is devoted to them—but they shouldn't be viewed as end products. Goals are useful only as they help us move from here toward somewhere else.

Like Alice, most of us think we want to go "somewhere," and it takes some experience to learn that, in life, there is no "somewhere." There is only the road to somewhere, and we are always on the way.

Where do we learn to think of life as having "somewheres," as having places that once we reach, we will be happy? Through the media. Much of what we know of life, we learn from television, plays, books, and movies; much of that is educational, sometimes in peculiarly useful ways. John Kenneth Galbraith, the Harvard professor whom President Kennedy appointed ambassador to India, reported in his book *Ambassador's Diary,* that when he arrived in India, he was expected to review a large contingent of Indian troops. He had no warning and no prior experience in reviewing troops. How did he know what to do? As he put it, "I drew heavily on old newsreels for my protocol . . ."

But, although the media have educated us in many ways, they have misled us into thinking that the world is full of endings, some happy, some sad, but always endings. The movie ends, the television show ends, the novel ends, the play ends. That is not the way the world is. In life there are no endings. No matter how pleasant or painful the weekend was, the cast always gets up on Monday morning and goes about its business. In the movie, the sun may set, the moon may rise, the honeymooners may walk hand in hand down the lane to a climactic fade-out; but in real life, the honeymooners will awaken to an average day that may start with the scratchy realization that here they are in this expensive resort with no toothbrushes and no toothpaste, and they can't get the taste of last night's dinner out of their mouths.

Drink, and dance and laugh and lie,
Love, the reeling midnight through,
For tomorrow we shall die!
(But, alas, we never do.)

Dorothy Parker, *The Flaw in Paganism*

To give up the concept of "endings" is one of the most important steps in learning to plan realistically. Many people have trouble accepting this, and maybe an example will help. One painful realization suffered by many young women who have aimed their lives toward happy endings ("a family, a nice home, and a good marriage") comes when the children leave home and they are left alone, when they realize the house that needs to be cleaned weekly is only a millstone around their necks, and when they see their husbands totally absorbed in their work, an absorption that may leave the wife excluded. For a woman in that position, happy endings are pretty flat.

The same thing happens to men; the scenario may be slightly different, but the outcome is the same. The quest for a simple "happy ending" eventually turns into frustration.

This sounds pessimistic only if you think life should be simple. Life is complicated—that's why it's fun—but we need a way of thinking about it that captures this complexity and that allows us to plan our goals accordingly.

Life is complicated—
that's why it's fun.

Think of life in this way. Instead of happy endings and "somewheres," think of life as a long, never-ending pathway stretching out ahead of you, with many other pathways leading off to either side. The pathway you are on now represents the life-style you are now living; the side pathways represent new directions you might take—new jobs, new hobbies, new places to live. One side pathway might be labeled "be a cartoonist," and if you have the proper talents and energy, you might choose to start down that pathway. Soon you would reach a fork where one branch would be labeled "free-lance cartoonist," and the other, "regularly employed." You will have to choose, and your choice will have considerable influence on your future options because the side pathways leading off the two branches will not always be the same.

*. . . think of life as a long,
never-ending pathway
stretching out ahead of you,
with many other pathways
leading off to the other side.*

Each side pathway has a gate, and the gate will be open for you only if you have the right credentials. Consequently, when you come to a side pathway, two factors will determine whether you will leave the pathway you are now on and start down a path leading in a new direction. The first factor is whether or not the gate is open to you, which will be determined by your credentials; the second factor is whether or not you want to go through the gate, even if it's open. The first factor—your credentials—is the more important because if the gate isn't open for you, you have no choice, no matter how badly you wish to follow the new pathway. Consequently, your main strategy in planning a life with maximum opportunities is to accumulate the best credentials possible—or, as I call them, assets—so that the maximum number of pathways will be open to you. You want the choice to be in your hands, not the gatekeepers' hands.

These pathways and gates are only imaginary, of course. They represent the choices you will have in life. They might be labeled with occupations: doctor, lawyer, merchant, chief; or with places to live: big city, small town, the country; or with general life-styles: married with large family, famous with lots of money, powerful politician, quiet life in the suburbs.

Whether or not a pathway will be open for you depends on your assets—that is, on factors such as your education, your experience, your skills, perhaps your family connections, or even your appearance. If you want to enter the pathway marked "medical school," for example, then you need to have taken the right courses in college, you need to have earned good grades, and you need to have impressed someone enough so that he or she will write a good letter of recommendation for you. If you want to go down the path marked "farming," then you'd better arrange to inherit a farm (or marry someone who will). If you want to live in Europe, then you need to have some job that is exportable, such as entertainer or scientist, or you need to speak a foreign language fluently, or you need to grow up in a family that has foreign connections, or you need a substantial amount of imagination, persistence, and luck. The point is, most pathways are open only to people with the right assets.

For most people the pathway ahead is a little misty. You cannot be exactly sure where your pathway is leading, and you certainly cannot see all possible side pathways that might appear in the future. Once you realize that the gates that will be open for you will depend on the assets you have, then—even if the future is misty—you can begin to increase your assets, even if you are not certain exactly which future pathways you will wish to follow. You will at least want to have the choice, and the more assets you have, the more pathways will open to you and the more choices you will have.

*For most people
the pathway ahead
is a little misty.*

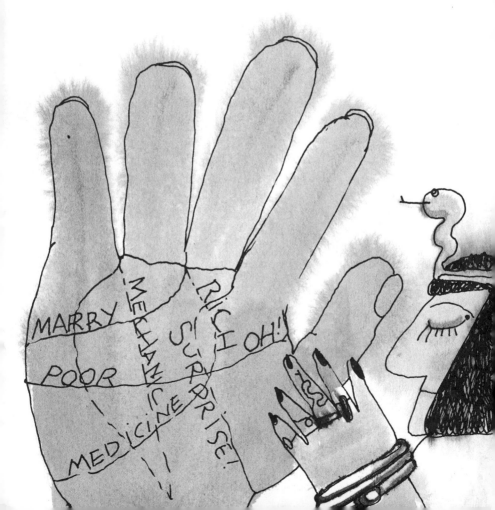

What opens new pathways? The next chapter is devoted totally to that question, and you should study it closely. Generally, what it says is that *education* opens new pathways, *experience* opens new pathways, *talents* open new pathways, *well-connected friends and family* open new pathways, *good health* opens new pathways (or at least keeps some from closing), and personal characteristics such as *intelligence, persistence,* and *good work habits* open new pathways.

Your age also has some impact on whether gateways will be open to you. Early in life, we start passing gateways leading off from our route and, unless we have the right assets and the desire to enter them early, some of them are forever closed to us. For example, the pathway "Be a concert pianist" comes along early in life, even as early as six years of age, and most of us shoot right by it without even realizing (or caring) that that pathway (i.e., that occupation) is probably forever closed to us. Some decisions have to be made quite early in life, although, remember, no decision is fixed. Even an early decision to devote yourself to the piano is only a decision to start down that pathway. Other pathways will continue to appear, some with open gates, some with locked gates, again depending on your credentials.

At the other extreme, some pathways don't come along until you've lived a while. Sometimes the restrictions are formal—you must be at least thirty-five years old to be President of the United States, for example—but generally the restrictions on age are more a matter of eliminating people without experience. Most influential politicians are in their fifties or sixties, not because of any formal restrictions, but because many years are required to build a political base.

There is no use in fretting much about your age; you can't change it, and you can't slow it down. What you can do is make certain that when you are old enough to consider entering a new pathway, you have the other credentials necessary for opening the gate—and that takes planning.

*There is no use
in fretting much about your age;
you can't change it . . .*

Planning

"If you want something to happen, make a space for it."

I once asked a successful man, while interviewing him about his career, "What led to your success? How did you make it to the top?"

"A lot of luck," he answered, "but a lot of planning, too. I've always been a planner."

"Tell me about that . . . when did you start planning?"

"I can tell you exactly when because I can remember it as if it were yesterday. I was in college, living in a dormitory with a boy from Iowa. He came in one night while a bunch of us were sitting around, talking about life. I could tell he was excited, but he didn't say anything until everyone else left. Then he blurted, 'My folks just got rich!! My mother called tonight—she walked out to the mailbox this morning and found a check for $89,000.'

"If you want something
to happen,
make a space for it."

26

"My reaction, after the initial astonishment, was only barely concealed envy. I asked him what it was all about.

"He said, 'I don't exactly understand, but I guess my dad bought some stock back in the depression and then forgot all about it. The company has just been sold, and this is his share.'"

My friend continued, "That night I lay in bed awake a long time, thinking. 'Why was it his family and not mine? Why him and not me?' Finally, I tried to analyze it in a systematic way.

"I thought to myself, 'What could possibly happen in my life to bring me such a windfall?' and bleakly I realized there was nothing. I had no old stock that would shoot up in value nor, as far as I was aware, did my family. I had no land where someone might suddenly find oil; I had no paintings that might turn out to be old masters; I had no talents that someone was going to miraculously discover overnight to make me famous—I had nothing going for me. And right there in the dormitory bed I said to myself, 'Charlie, if you want something like that to happen in your life, you've got to plant some seeds, and you'd better plant a lot of them, 'cause you can't tell which ones will sprout.' Since then I have always been a planter of seeds. A few of them have sprouted, and here I am."

More recently, a university student put it to me more succinctly. This girl, a likable, alert, enthusiastic type, said to me, "If you want something to happen in your life, Professor, you've got to make a space for it." She put her hands straight out in front of her, palms together, and started forcing them slowly apart, as though she had stuck them into a bale of cotton and was slowly forcing it apart, making a bigger and bigger space. "You see, you've got to make a space for it ... for whatever it is that you want."

Both of these people were planners; they made things happen in their lives, either by planting seeds or by pushing apart the cotton. They didn't sit passively, waiting for life to come along; they went out looking. They made plans.

Here are some comments that should help you make better plans.

1 *Planning is a matter of probabilities,* which means that sometimes your plans will turn out and sometimes they won't—you will save yourself a lot of grief by realizing that sooner rather than later. Nothing is a sure thing, and any plans that you make for the future have to deal with uncertainty. Once you realize that, several other conclusions are apparent. *First,* there are probably things you can do to raise your probabilities for success. *Second,* you had better have some alternatives in case your first plan doesn't work out. *Third,* any given plan can fail, and you had best prepare for that possibility also.

*. . . you've got to plant some seeds,
and you'd better plant a lot of them,
'cause you can't tell which ones
will sprout.*

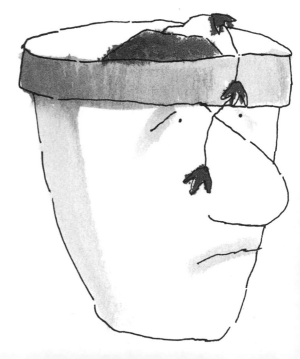

2 *Your planning should cover different time spans,* such as one hour, one week, one year, or ten years. Obviously, planning has to be much different if you are thinking about next year as opposed to ten years from now. You can, and should, plan ten years ahead, but you cannot do it with much precision because there are too many uncertain factors. As Winston Churchill once said when speaking of planning the affairs of the British Empire, "One must always look ahead, but it is difficult to look farther than one can see." You can, and should, plan for one hour ahead also; you can do that with substantial precision, but of course, any one single hour won't have much impact on your life.

Although there will be much uncertainty in your life over the next ten years, one thing that you can count on with absolute certainty is that ten years from now you will be ten years older. If you are reading this book at age seventeen, in the next ten years of your life you will probably complete your education, you will probably leave home, you will probably marry, you will probably start your first job, you will probably (according to the average) switch jobs at least once. The odds on all of those things happening are high; what planning are you doing about them?

If you are reading this book at age thirty-seven, in the next ten years you will probably reach your peak in your occupational life, your income will probably reach a maximum and level off, your children will probably be reaching college age and leaving home, your body will be aging more rapidly, and you will probably have less energy and endurance than you have now. You will be well on your way to middle age. Distressing, perhaps, but a fact, and one that you should plan for.

You can categorize your goals roughly as follows:

---

long-range goals

---

medium-range goals

---

short-range goals

---

mini-goals

---

micro-goals

Long-range goals are those concerned with the overall style of life that you wish to live—the type of job you want, whether or not you wish to be married, the kind of family that you want, the general situation that you wish to live in.

Although you should develop some overall idea of what you are after, don't try to plan long-range goals in detail, because too many changes will come along. Have an overall plan, but keep it flexible.

Medium-range goals are goals covering the next five years or so; they cover the particular kind of training or education you are seeking, or the next step in your career. You have more control over these goals, and you can tell along the way whether you are going to achieve them and modify your efforts accordingly.

Short-range goals are goals covering the period from about one month to one year from now. You can set these goals quite realistically and can tell fairly soon whether or not you are reaching them. Don't set impossible goals for yourself. While you always want to stretch yourself, you don't want to become discouraged. Aim realistically, but try hard to achieve your aims.

*"One must always look ahead,
but it is difficult to look farther
than one can see."*

Mini-goals are those goals covering from about one day to one month. You have much more control over these goals than you do over the longer-term goals. You can plan a program for the next week, or the next month, and your chances of carrying it out— assuming your plans were reasonable—are good. Or, if you find you planned too ambitiously, you can modify it for the period after that. By thinking in shorter hunks of time, you have far more control over each hunk.

Micro-goals are goals covering the next fifteen minutes to an hour. Realistically, these are the only goals that you have direct control over. Because of this direct control, micro-goals, even though they are modest in impact, are extraordinarily important in your life, for it is only through these micro-goals that you can attain your larger goals. As the old adage says, "A journey of a thousand miles begins with a single step." If you don't make any progress toward your long-range goals in the next fifteen minutes, when will you? The following fifteen minutes? The fifteen minutes after that? Sooner or later, you have to pick fifteen minutes and get going.

If you plan your micro-goals well, and then make progress toward them—"I'm going to start that term paper right now," "I'm going to learn that new technique right now," "I'm going to make that call right now"—your long-range goals will take care of themselves.

In general, the bigger the goal, the less control you have over achieving it. If, for example, one of your long-range goals is to become a famous pianist, there's very little you can do about that today—you can't go out and brew up a little instant fame. In contrast, you have a lot more control over micro-goals. You can say to yourself, "In the next hour I am going to master one line of this Beethoven sonata," and you can do it. One mastered line will not make you famous, but it's a step—and a necessary one—in the right direction.

The point is that the only kind of planning you have direct control over are the modest, little goals; the trick of planning a successful life is to stack together these smaller goals in a way that increases your chances of reaching the long-range goals you really care about.

3 *Plan for intensity;* in at least one area of your life, be intense. Focus strongly on something, whether it is your job, a hobby, or some group activity. Be good at something, good enough so that you can take quiet pride in knowing that you are a valuable person, that you can do at least one thing well. To do this requires dedication, determination, and persistence. You cannot be dedicated and determined and persistent in all areas; don't try it, but do pick one area and excel. If you pick the right area—and the next chapter has a lot to say about that—good things will happen to you.

4 *Plan some diversity in your life,* even while you are focusing on one area. Life is full of changes, and the best protection against catastrophic change is diversity in your talents, in your assets. In your planning pay attention to this fact.

5 *Plan for gradual improvement,* not spectacular leaps. Practically everything worthwhile in life is achieved in small steps. Education is accumulated gradually, babies grow up a day at a time, beautiful gardens are designed and grown slowly; talents are honed, relationships are forged, deep affection is created, all very gradually. Each of our lives is a series of gradual campaigns in all areas— job, family, friends—to make a better life, and few campaigns move quickly.

Nature provides many guidelines here. A slow and steady stream of water will, in time, erode the hardest rock; a small, insignificant sprout will, in time, slowly and imperceptibly turn into a mighty oak; almost unnoticed, a child will, in time, grow up to be an independent adult. Recognize the gradualness of life and the power of "in time."

A final comment on planning: To plan, you must have information. You must know something about the subject of your plans. If you are trying to plan your schooling, you must know something about the educational options available to you. If you are trying to plan your occupational future, you must know something about jobs. If you are trying to plan your future home, you must know something about housing and real estate. To accumulate this knowledge, you have to do some digging. You have to read books, pamphlets, magazines, anything relevant that you can get your hands on. You have to talk to knowledgeable people, a wide range of them. You have to accumulate some life experiences for yourself. Virtually anything that educates you is worthwhile, so seek out some experiences in the areas in which you are trying to plan.

The basic point is, you can't make good plans until you have some raw material to plan with. You need knowledge and experience.

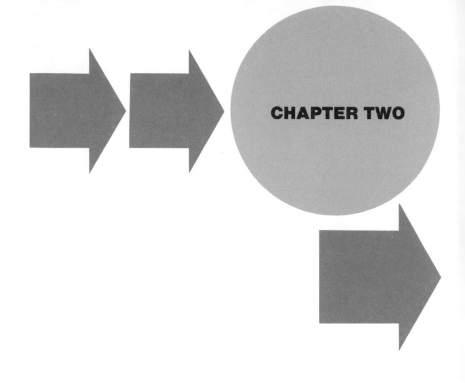

CHAPTER TWO

*For unto every one that hath shall be given,
and he shall have abundance:
but from him that hath not shall be taken away
even that which he hath.*

Matthew 25:29

If You Have It, Use It

To be able to live the kind of life you want, you need to have as many choices open to you as possible. To make choices, you must have assets—you must have something going for you. Assets include such things as good health, a good education, a wide array of talents, broadening experiences, and helpful family and friends. Even if you don't know exactly what you want out of life, you can concentrate now on building your assets because the more you accumulate, the more choices you will eventually have, no matter what direction you choose to go.

You can evaluate your assets in much the same way as a corporation does: add up your strong points and subtract your weak ones. The only difference is that you should be looking at your psychological assets while a corporation usually looks at dollars. In the following paragraphs various kinds of psychological assets are discussed. As you read about them, take stock of your own situation—what assets do you have? Which ones are under your control and thus can be increased? Once again, the more assets you have now, the more options you will have later.

The assets that are going to have the greatest impact on your future choices are:

    I Your talents and skills
  II Your intelligence
 III Your motivation
  IV Your friends
   V Your education
  VI Your family
 VII Your experiences
VIII Your appearance
  IX Your health

The more you have going for you in each of these categories, the more choices you will have in life.

I Your Talents and Skills

Your talents and skills are important ingredients in opening up new pathways for you. *Talents* include general abilities such as musical, mathematical, or athletic talent. *Skills* include specific abilities such as playing the piano, programming a computer, or playing tennis.

In a crude way, you can think of *talents* as naturally given, *skills* as something you work to acquire. The most effective approach for any one person is to discover where his or her talents lie, then work to develop skills in that area.

If, for example, you have a talent for getting along with many different types of people, you should concentrate on developing skills useful for working with people—i.e., planning and running meetings, straightening out disputes between groups, motivating people to work as a team.

If your talents are in the artistic area, you should concentrate on learning specific skills such as sketching pictures, molding clay, or working with metals.

Talents are the guidelines for developing your skills, but the skills themselves are more important in expanding your options. If you can play the guitar, or operate a shortwave radio, or grow orchids, or sell things door-to-door, or write short stories, you will have more options in your life than will people who cannot do anything special.

Some skills are obviously worth more than others; other things being equal, you should spend your time acquiring the more valuable ones. How can you decide which ones are valuable? Here are some guidelines:

1 *Is the skill part of some occupation?* Writing, for example, is a major part of many jobs—newspaper reporter, public relations representative, research scientist, business executive. The ability to write well is a necessity in any job that involves communicating with others. Consequently, it is a useful skill to develop.

Similarly, the ability to work with tools is an important skill on many jobs. If you can weld, or solder, or run a power saw, or float cement, or run a diesel engine, or install plumbing, then you have a skill that may give you a head start. The more skills you have, the better your chances; any skill that can open up a job for you is valuable.

Don't set impossible goals
for yourself.

Of course, you don't have to enter an occupation just because you are skilled in it—if you learn to operate woodworking equipment, you don't have to be a carpenter. The point is, if you have that skill, you will likely have more choices. For example, if you do have some woodworking skills, you might be asked to help with the construction of a theater stage set, and that opportunity might open up an entire new set of possibilities for you.

2 *Will other people pay you to teach them the skill?* In deciding which skills are valuable, look around you. What skills are people paying for? If someone will pay you to teach them your skill, one advantage is obvious— you can make some money as a teacher. There are even more important advantages. As a teacher, you will come to the attention of more people, and as a consequence, other benefits may fall into your lap. If you are teaching photography at the local Y and some businessman in your class likes your work, he may think of you the next time he sends a photographer on a foreign assignment. A long shot? Sure, all good things are.

Another important result of teaching is that it builds your self-confidence. To teach others, you must be good enough to be considered an expert. The more such opportunities you have, the more self-assurance you will develop; the more self-assurance you have, the more opportunities you will find. A pleasant cycle.

3 *Will the skill be useful throughout life?*
Regrettably, many of the skills that we develop as children are merely that—childish skills. Knowing how to work a yo-yo, play pool, throw a Frisbee, or build sand castles are not very useful skills for adults. I am not putting down yo-yos, pool tables, Frisbees, or sand castles; I have spent many fine hours with them. But long hours of practice are best devoted elsewhere.

You needn't be continually serious; occasionally, everyone should play with mud pies, or blow soap bubbles, or lie on the ground and look at clouds, but do these activities for the joy of the moment—a marvelously worthwhile goal—not because they are going to lead to useful, satisfying work.

If you are going to spend hours and hours during your youth acquiring some skill, work on something that will be useful to you throughout your life. Athletics offers some useful examples. Although many students spend a fantastic amount of time practicing athletic skills, those skills are not especially worthwhile later in life. Adults do not often play team sports such as basketball or football, partially because these sports are physically rough and our eagerness to participate in them drops off quickly past age twenty-five, partially because older people seldom have access to the necessary facilities, and partially because team sports require a lot of people to play them at the same time and adults have busy schedules.

Individual sports, such as golf, tennis, hand-ball, and swimming, are more popular among adults. Consequently, students would be wise to learn some of these "carry-over" sports rather than restricting themselves to team sports.

Team sports do offer other advantages: the thrill of organized competition, the feeling of belonging to a close-knit unit, the discipline of living up to the expectations of others. Young people need these experiences, especially to help their sense of belonging with their peers. Team sports have their place.

As people grow older, team sports become less important, and many people find to their dismay that they have no carry-over athletic skills. And, as adults fear failure more than young people do, most adults won't risk new learning experiences. You will likely feel the same way when you grow older, so learn some skills now that will be useful to you later on.

. . . the bigger the goal,
the less control you have
over achieving it.

4 *Will the skill help you conquer new environments and gain new experiences?* The more different settings you are familiar with, the more options you will have, the more gateways that will be open to you down the long pathway ahead.

If you can think and speak on your feet, you will be called upon more often to lead discussions, or give speeches, or organize new activities.

If you can take and develop excellent photographs, you will have more opportunities for fun and excitement in photographing sports events, or flamboyant social events, or visiting dignitaries.

If you can speak French, German, or any foreign language, you are more likely to meet people from that country, or even to travel there yourself. If the Russian gymnastics team comes to town and you are the only person around who speaks Russian, you are *very* likely to be invited to the reception; in fact, you will probably be put in charge—and, with luck, the Russians will invite you for a return visit.

If you can sail and do celestial navigation, you are more likely to be asked to crew on an oceangoing sailboat.

If you can fix small engines, radios, and other gadgets, you are more likely to find work in a research laboratory, or even to go along on research expeditions such as snowmobile trips to the North Pole or Jeep trips deep into Africa.

To be lucky, you need skills.

5 *Do you like to do it?* In selecting a skill to develop, pick something that you like to do, because if you don't like it, you're never going to be really good at it. Determination can take you a long way; sometimes you can learn to like a disagreeable activity by sticking with it until you're good at it, but that is an exception. If you don't like to do something, work on something else.

This assumes that you can find something you like. If nothing appeals to you, if you've never done anything that excited you, if you can't think of any interesting people to imitate, if you are continually passive, unimaginative, and bored with life, then this book can't help you—probably nothing will.

But . . . if you are serious about wanting to try new activities, to learn new skills, and to have new experiences, but don't know how to begin, here are some suggestions:

1 Read magazines—art magazines, electronic magazines, travel magazines, financial magazines, scientific magazines, car magazines—you can find them at the drugstore or at the library.

2 Do what other interesting people do—watch them or, better yet, ask them; they will tell you.

. . . in at least
one area of your life,
be intense.

3 Spend some money on some new things—buy a leather kit, or a clock kit, or some new plants.

4 Visit a factory, or a museum, or a botanical garden; they're all filled with people being paid to do interesting things.

5 Browse hobby shops.

6 Volunteer for something—work in a hospital, or a prison, or a school.

7 Ask other people to explain their hobbies or their jobs to you. Most people are delighted to talk about themselves, particularly if you can ask intelligent questions. Find out what other people do that interests them.

II Your Intelligence

The word *intelligence* has been used for many years by psychologists to label those talents that the person on the street calls "brainpower." Generally, it means the person's ability to cope with the world—how bright he or she is.

Most students sooner or later have an opportunity to take intelligence tests in school—sometimes they are called aptitude tests, or scholastic ability tests, or tests of mental abilities—so people usually have some notion of where they stand in relation to the general population. This is important information, but unfortunately it is sometimes misused. When you have this information about yourself, you should use it, but you should not exaggerate its importance.

For the most part, intelligence tests measure your ability to handle abstract concepts, that is, your ability to see and analyze relationships between different classes of things such as words, or numbers, or ideas. This ability, which is important for success in most college subjects, especially science and math, is only one of the many possible mental abilities. Whether you score high or low on an intelligence test does not automatically mean you will be a success or a failure. Other abilities, especially imagination and persistence, are at least as important as intelligence.

Intelligence and its relation to success in life is about the same as height and its relation to success in playing basketball. Height is an enormous asset if you are a basketball player; the more of it the better. But simply being tall is no guarantee that you will be a star. To be an outstanding player, you must not only be tall, you must be in good condition, you must have good coaching, and you must practice, practice, practice. Thus, it is the same with intelligence and success. To be bright, that is, to be intelligent, is an enormous benefit, but that alone will not automatically bring you success unless you are (1) willing to exercise your intelligence (get in good condition), (2) seek out good teaching (coaching), and (3) are willing to practice, practice, practice.

Another point: Many good basketball players are not particularly tall; they succeed through some other talent such as quickness or unusual dexterity ("good hands"), or through fantastic determination and hard work. In the same way, many people with modest intelligence, as measured by the tests, can be successful. This doesn't mean that the tests are no good; it means that there are other talents besides intelligence that are important.

Can you improve your intelligence? Can you raise your IQ? Within limits, there is not much you can do after your childhood days to increase your IQ. (Whether the development of intelligence in young children can be accelerated is still an open question. Apparently, if children in their early years, say under age eight, are given a great deal of stimulation through books, imaginative television programs, nature trips, visits to museums, factories, offices, and laboratories, their mental processes will be better developed than those of children who are deprived of such stimulation.)

*. . . the best protection
against catastrophic change
is diversity in your talents . . .*

After about age fifteen or sixteen, the rate of mental development slows, and a person's standing compared with others on measures of intelligence remains about the same for many years. Still, all is not lost; even though your IQ does not grow much past age sixteen, it can always be put in better shape, just as your body can always be better conditioned. Some people take good care of their bodies: they exercise regularly, they eat the proper diet, they don't smoke or drink to excess. Consequently, their bodies, when called upon to perform, do much better than do the bodies of people who don't take care of them.

The same is true of intelligence. During our teenage years, our intelligence—in terms of power to handle abstract concepts—reaches the general level where it will remain for the rest of our lives, but, like our bodies, we can either let it deteriorate through lack of use (and as a result be disappointed when we have to call upon it) or keep it sharp by constant stimulation.

The best way to keep your intelligence in condition is to stay active mentally. Keep reading, studying, taking courses, exposing yourself to others who are better educated than yourself, tackling new challenges. These activities all help keep your brain from getting rusty.

If you know your IQ, you should use this information to help you make a sensible occupational choice. Generally, the more complex the occupation, then the higher your IQ must be to succeed there. People in the most complex occupations—nuclear physicists, medical researchers, federal judges, high-level accountants, university professors—are drawn from the highest levels of intelligence, say the top 15 percent. A few people from lower down on the ladder succeed in these occupations, but only because they have other assets such as the willingness to work unbelievably hard, or an unusual imagination, or family connections, or occasionally pure luck.

Below this elite corps is a much larger group of people drawn from perhaps the upper 30 percent of the population; here are the doctors, lawyers, accountants, psychologists, business executives, ministers, social workers, engineers, biologists, chemists, military officers, and other such professionals.

Below these come the majority of people, those of average intelligence. The majority of us are average, although this may be hard to accept; no one likes to be considered "only average." Yet this is inevitable, because the definition of "average" means the place where most people fall. Being average should not depress anyone, because even those of us who are most average have a lot of control over our lives. As the famous black athlete Satchel Paige said, "Ain't no man that can avoid being born average, but ain't nobody got to be common."

Most of the workers in our society have a normal amount of intelligence, that is, an average amount of intelligence. Those who work in offices, in hospitals, on farms; those who drive trucks, who are policemen, beauticians, salespeople, or owners of small businesses—on measures of intelligence these people generally fall into the normal range. There are many exceptions. Some people in these occupations score very high on intelligence tests, which means either that they have not had the opportunity to move into better jobs or that they have not stretched themselves enough. Other people in these jobs score quite low on tests of intelligence, which means either that they have had unusual opportunities handed to them or that they have applied themselves with unusual dedication, climbing farther up the ladder than have others at the same level of intelligence.

Plan for gradual improvement,
not spectacular leaps. . . .
A slow and steady stream of water
will, in time,
erode the hardest rock . . .

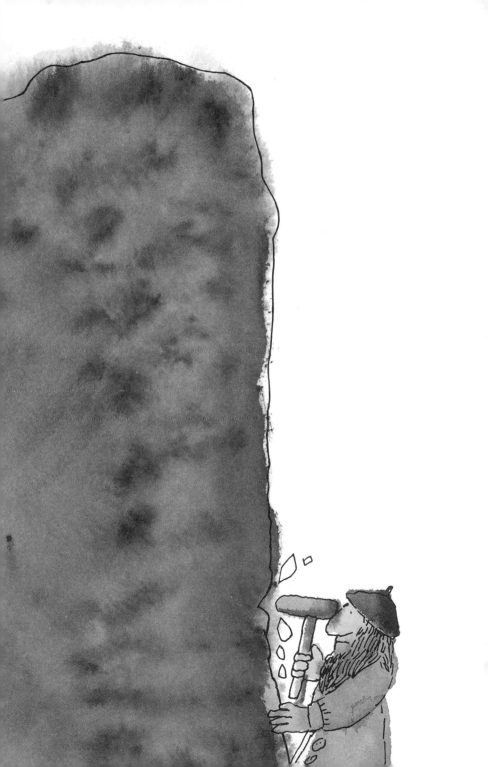

People with lower scores on measures of intelligence, those below average, usually end up in less complicated jobs such as factory work, janitorial work, simple clerical positions, or a wide range of other unskilled jobs. They make useful contributions and they usually enjoy their work, but they do not have to deal with the same complexity as do those in higher-level jobs, and of course they are paid much less. Even at this modest level of intelligence, people differ a great deal in their imagination, enthusiasm, and dedication to work, and people with modest intelligence who have these traits frequently contribute a great deal through their work.

So, remember these three things about your brainpower:

1 If you have it, use it or you will lose it.
2 Aim realistically for a level at which you can succeed.
3 Even if you score low, there are other ways to win.

III Your Motivation

How hard are you willing to work? How persistent are you? How badly do you want to do well?

These are questions of motivation. No matter how smart or talented you are, no matter how many opportunities you have, if you are not motivated, you will probably not accomplish much, which means you won't have many choices in life. No accomplishments, no choices.

What motivates people? How can you increase your own motivation? Psychologists have been studying these questions for many years and have some, but by no means all, of the answers.

Here are some of the basic findings:

1 Different people are motivated by different things. Some people want to make lots of money, some people want to make great scientific discoveries, some people want to help others, some people want to create artistic things. Activities that seem incredibly stimulating to one person are totally boring to another. Consequently, the secret is to find those activities that attract you, because you will never be particularly motivated until you find an activity that is important to you.

2 One motivation that seems important to almost everyone is the feeling that they are doing something worthwhile. No one likes to feel that their work is worthless, that no one else appreciates them. Consequently, find something to do that you think is worth doing.

3 The more that people understand the value of what they are doing, the more motivated they are to do it well. Similarly, the better they understand what their individual rewards will be, that is, "what's in it for them," the more motivated they will be.

. . . occasionally,
everyone should play
with mud pies . . .

This is an important point, worth stressing. Many times students are not aware of the benefits of doing well so they do not try hard. "What's the point of getting good grades?" they say. "I'm never going to use this stuff again."

Sometimes they are right, but usually they simply don't understand why what they are learning will eventually be important. If you are a student, don't be shortsighted. Look ahead. The better you understand the demands of adult life, the more you will understand why practically all learning is important.

4 People tend to be consistent in their level of motivation; for example, those students who do well in high school tend to be those who will do well in college, who in turn tend to be those who do well in advanced study such as law or medicine, or in graduate school. People who do well in one task tend to do well in others; people who do well in one job tend to do well in others.

There is substantial consistency in human performance, and, to the extent that you can, you should try to succeed in whatever you attempt. Success tends to become habitual.

5 One of the most important and well-established psychological findings is that we tend to perform at about the same level as those people who are close to us. Groups of people working together set up informal norms of performance, and these norms are reinforced, usually in subtle ways, by the group members. Workers on an assembly line, for example, usually reach an understanding, usually unstated, of how much work they consider fair. Any worker who gets overeager and tries to exceed the norms is subtly disciplined by the group. "Rate-busters," as they are sometimes known, are brought into line so that they do not embarrass the rest of the group by showing them up.

The same phenomenon occurs in many other groups. Among students, doing too well is sometimes looked upon with great distrust. In some groups, a person is supposed to be happy with a "gentleman's C," the implication being that anyone working for a better grade is no gentleman. A whole vocabulary has grown up to describe this student; the words change with new generations of students, but the sentiment is constant—"apple-polisher," "curve-raiser," "brownnoser."

The same situation exists in the world of work. People in different settings have different expectations of themselves and their coworkers. In some places people expect a great deal from each other; they stimulate each other, they encourage each other, they urge each other on to greater heights of achievement. In other settings people hold each other down by tolerating shoddy work, or by not expecting much of each other.

The implication for you as an individual is that you ought to seek out a place where you will be encouraged to achieve—assuming, of course, that achievement is important to you. You should seek out those situations where you will be stimulated, not deadened. Usually, this means finding people who are better than you and trying to raise yourself to their level.

The basic point is that the people you work with are going to have a substantial impact on your motivation. If you want to be motivated to achieve, the choice of your coworkers may be the most important choice you make. Stay away from the rumdums; they will drag you down.

"Ain't no man
that can avoid being born average,
but ain't nobody got to be common."

IV Your Friends

Along with your coworkers, your friends are going to be an important factor in your life, especially in what you will accomplish and the choices you will have open to you.

Parents are always worried about the kinds of friends their children have, and sometimes the children feel overprotected. But what the parents know now, and what you will eventually learn, is that hardly anything influences our lives as much as the people we associate with. There are many reasons for this, but one of the most important is that we continually use other people for models; that is, we use them as guides for our own actions, and close friends prove to be some of our most powerful models.

Consequently, look around you. The general life that you are going to have will probably be similar to the life that your friends are living, partially because you will, consciously or unconsciously, model your life after theirs. If your friends are too young to have a definite life-style, then look at the parents of your friends. They offer the best prediction of the kind of life that you will be living in a few years. The prediction is far from perfect, but it is the best one you can make now.

No matter what group you choose to associate with over the next several years, you will become more like the members of that group in your attitudes, actions, and opinions. (They will become more like you, too; the influence works in both directions.) A specific example: A young man who is majoring, say, in art and who moves into a dormitory dominated by students majoring in another subject, say, science, will tend to change his attitudes in the scientific direction. He may even change his major to science. If he lives in the dorm for a long time, he will likely develop more positive feelings toward science than will art students who only associate with other art students. Over time, the minority tends to change to become like the majority. The changes are not necessarily large and are by no means certain, but the general tendency is there, and it will happen to you, too. Over the years you are going to change to become more like the majority of your friends, and they will change to become more like you.

Again, an important implication is that you had better choose your friends fairly carefully because this is one way of controlling your own behavior. By putting yourself in close contact with people whom you would like to be like, you are apt to change in ways that will please you.

Conversely, if you associate with people with problems, you are likely to find yourself with problems, too. If your friends are a bunch of losers, if they are always in trouble with the law, if they are fat and out of shape, if they never have any money, if they are frequently drunk, or smoke a lot, or use hard drugs, if they constantly have trouble in school, if they waste hours each day watching television, if they try to solve most of their problems by "being tough," then you are likely to slide into those same patterns. Through these kinds of friends you can pick up a significant number of liabilities and very few assets. The ancient adage "Birds of a feather flock together" is well supported by psychological research.

Fortunately, the other side of the coin is also true. If your friends are talented, if they get good grades, if they are thoughtful toward others, if they are good athletes and keep their bodies in shape, if they handle alcohol, tobacco, and other drugs reasonably, if they are happy, if they are involved in healthy pursuits such as singing, dancing, athletics, environmental programs, scientific contests, useful hobbies, or good jobs, then you are more likely to become involved in the same activities.

Although these comments are geared to students, the same factors operate throughout life. Whether you are seventeen, thirty-seven, or sixty-seven, your friends are going to have a sizable impact on you, especially in establishing your attitudes and opinions. If you mainly socialize with Republicans, you are going to think more and more like a Republican; if you spend time with people who value exercise and good health, you are going to keep yourself in better health; if you spend time with people who travel, you will inevitably travel more; if you spend time with people who complain about their lot in life, you will likely be a complainer yourself; if you spend time

with people who contribute in worthwhile ways to our society, you yourself are likely to contribute also.

These are only probabilistic statements; each of them should be prefaced with the phrase, "the chances are that ...," but the trends are fairly strong. Good friends can be wonderful assets; poor ones can set you back for years.

One other thing you should know about friends. The people who do best with friends are the people who need them least. If you need your friends as a crutch, if you constantly lean on other people and cannot stand upright on your own, if you take from friendships more than you give, you will not be a welcome addition to most circles. Regrettably, in this as in so many other areas, those who need friends the most will have the fewest.

V Your Education

*Genius without education
is like silver in the mine.*

Benjamin Franklin

One reason education is so important to you is that it creates many of the other assets listed earlier. If you have a good education, you automatically accumulate useful skills, broadening experiences, and stimulating friends. Consequently, when planning your career, pay a great deal of attention to education, for it is a wonderful way to increase your options. (And, for most people it's a lot of fun. Many people will tell you that the years they spent in school were the best years of their lives.)

There are three particular points that you should pay attention to in seeking an advanced education.

First, *you should study something that you enjoy.* If you are having trouble deciding what that is, give yourself a few years to try out several areas. Take some solid, basic courses—science, mathematics, business, history, art—in which you will learn a lot about many fields; especially choose courses that will build your assets. A good school counselor can help you decide which courses will be good, no matter what you eventually decide to do. Hopefully, this book will give you some ideas also. Generally, the more rigorous the course, such as science or math, the more useful it will be later on in expanding your options.

Don't worry if you haven't yet found an area that excites you; many people take several years to settle in. But do worry about trying new, diverse areas. Keep experimenting with new fields; don't just sit on your hands.

Second, *you should go to the best educational institution that you can afford to and that you can get into.* There are several advantages in going to a good school: (a) You will probably get a better education; (b) you

*No one likes to feel
that their work
is worthless . . .*

will be surrounded by capable, stimulating people, and as we have already seen, the quality of people that you associate with is going to have a lot to do with the kind of person you become; and (c) the reputation of the school that you attend is going to affect the pathways that eventually open up to you. A degree from Harvard is going to give you more options than a degree from Southwest State Teachers College, unfair as that may seem.

Third, *wherever you go, you should try to do well.* Again, the better your grades, the more options you will have later. Further, and more important, if you don't learn to discipline yourself in school (assuming, now, that you are studying something that you enjoy), you may not be able to discipline yourself later.

Curiously, this last point—doing well in school—may be more important than the second point—going to a good school. Students who earn outstanding records in medio-cre schools do as well or better in life as do

Success tends to become habitual.

average students from the best schools. I saw this demonstrated vividly when I was on the faculty of the University of Minnesota. When we studied the performance of the valedictorians from all Minnesota high schools, we found that the top students from the average high schools in the state did better at the university than did average students from the best high schools. When the Bell Telephone system did a study of their young executives, they found the same result; those who had graduated in the top third of their class from average colleges were doing as well as or better than executives who had graduated in the middle of their class at the most prestigious universities. One likely explanation of these results is that success becomes habit-forming. Good students in mediocre schools learn to do well, and they learn to expect top performance from themselves. When they move on into other settings, they continue to expect top performance from themselves.

VI Your Family

While you are young, your family has more impact on you than any other factor in your life. Even when you are older, the family's influence is still strong. Most of us vote the same way as our parents, go to the same church as our parents, eat the same kinds of food as our parents, and on and on. In many ways, we are what our parents are.

Your family influences your other assets, and can be an important asset in itself. Family connections can open doors, family skills can be passed down from generation to generation, families can provide experiences for their children, such as travel, that would be impossible for the children to have otherwise.

Some people get along better with their parents than others, and you may be one who thinks your family is not much of an asset. You may be right . . . or you may just need more perspective. As Mark Twain said, "When I was a boy of fourteen, I thought my father was one of the stupidest mortals to walk the face of the earth; when I turned twenty-one, I was amazed to see how much the old gentleman had learned in seven years." We all go through the phase of rejecting our parents and wishing we had been born into another family. When that happens to you, try to realize that the other family you want to be born into is probably having the same troubles you are.

The purpose of this book is to encourage you to look at your situation systematically and to act to improve your assets. Where your family is involved, how can you do that? How can you use your family to increase your skills, or your motivation, or your education?

There are several ways.

First, ask them. What are their ideas? You might be surprised at how helpful your parents can be, if you give them the opportunity.

Second, learn whatever skills they can teach you. If they can cook, or adjust carburetors, or program computers, or do macramé, or operate ham radios, or understand the stock market, you've got a wonderful resource right in your own home. Tap it.

Third, utilize whatever material assets are available. Some families, because of their financial holdings, can make more opportunities available for their children than their children would otherwise have. An obvious and extreme case is that of the parents who pass on a farm to their children; without such a boost, most young farmers would have a great deal of trouble getting started. Look into that possibility in your own family. If your family is in business, study the business thoroughly before you decide whether or not you want to continue it. In particular, don't reject it until you understand everything that is involved. You may have more opportunities under your nose than you understand.

If you do inherit something worthwhile from your family—whether it be money, or a business, or land, or simply a famous name—

. . . we tend to perform at about the same level as those people who are close to us.

recognize those resources for exactly what they are, that is, available assets that you can use to expand your own choices. But recognize also that family assets can be a burden, especially if you confuse them with *your own assets* as a person. Through the years, as a psychologist, I have worked with many people who have inherited money or fame, and I have seen the many problems it can cause. The people who handle it best are those who have honest, solid accomplishments of their own, independent of family help. They have a much better sense of who they are and what they can do than do those who have traded on only family assets.

When I talk now with young people who are facing the prospects of inheriting a large fortune, or a famous name, or of being overshadowed by an incredibly talented father or mother, I recommend strongly that they cut loose for a few years and prove to themselves that they can make it on their own. After they have achieved that self-assurance, they can then walk back into the family circle, secure in the knowledge that they could get along without the family resources if they had to. Without such confidence, family assets can become oppressive. If your name is Kennedy, or Rockefeller, or Vanderbilt, or your community's equivalent, you are going to have a lot of trouble establishing your identity as an independent individual, valuable in your own right, so you had better put that goal of independence near the top of your list.

Fourth, and most important, whatever else you do with your family, use them as an introduction to at least two occupations, that is, the ones your parents are in. To understand what an occupation is all about is difficult for an outsider, almost impossible, but at least your parents can help you understand theirs.

To help you get your parents (or your aunts, uncles, grandparents, neighbors, or teachers) to talk about their jobs, here are some questions you can ask. Almost *everyone* likes to talk about his or her work to someone who is really interested, so don't be bashful about asking.

1 How did you happen to choose this occupation?
   Many people will answer, "Oh, just by chance—it was an accident." Ignore that. While luck plays some part in occupational choice, other factors, which the people may not understand themselves, are usually more important. When people are explaining to you how they first started in an occupation, try to analyze what assets they had going for them. What choices did they really have?

2 What do you like best about it?

3 What don't you like?

4 What kind of people tend to do well in your job?

5 Do you do the same thing all day long, or is there a lot of variety?

6 How much money does the average worker in this job make?

   You should not ask people how much money they make; they will consider that rude. But you can ask them how much their coworkers make, and they will usually answer freely.

7 What kind of people do you work with? Do you like them?

   For most of us one of the main determinants of whether we enjoy our work or not is the people we work with. Pay some attention to that fact when you are looking for work.

8 Can you think of some particular event that happened recently on your job that made you feel particularly good? Can you tell me about it? Why did it make you feel good?

9 Can you tell me about something that made you feel bad? What was the problem?

10 What does the future look like? Will there be good opportunities for someone like me?

Try out these questions on your parents. You will probably find that you are a better interviewer than you think, and you will learn a lot about both your parents and their work.

After you gain some confidence from talking with them, start asking other adults these questions. The better informed you are, the better choices you will make.

VII Your Experiences

Among your most important assets are your experiences; if you plan them with some foresight, you can gain a variety of experience with little cost. (That is, little cost in dollars, but you may pay in other ways; as a Presbyterian minister once said, "Experience may not be worth what it costs, but I can't seem to get it for any less.") Whatever they cost, experiences can never be taken away from you.

Experiences happen haphazardly in life; you meet people, you travel places, you try new ways, you grow older. Yet you can also plan your experiences, and you should organize them so that you learn the maximum from them. Don't let things "just happen"; let them happen in a way that helps you know more about life afterward than you did before.

When you are trying to plan your career, for example, you should accumulate as many job experiences as possible, especially when you are young and can explore different possibilities fairly easily. Try out a variety of jobs, work in many different settings, volunteer while you're still in high school for different tasks. The more you learn now, the better informed your decisions will be later.

In the next chapter six basic types of jobs are discussed. Here's a brief preview of them now, along with some ways you can gain some experience in each type. These experiences can help you make better choices later and, equally important, they can teach you skills that will be useful later. The more experiences you have, especially those that teach you new skills, the more options you will have later in life. And the reverse is true: if you have no experiences, no skills, you are not going to have many future choices.

Realistic, practical, mechanical jobs

In this type of job, people work mainly with tools. Specific jobs include carpenter, farmer, X-ray technician, engineer, laboratory technician. For a summer, find a job as an apprentice to a skilled craftsman such as a carpenter or

Don't let things
"just happen" . . .

a plumber, or work on a farm. If you live in a city, volunteer to help the stage electrician in a community theater; such places need your help badly, and although you probably won't be paid, you will learn a lot about electrical work. Work in a gas station, but don't be satisfied with the routine work of pumping gas. Hang around while people are working on engines and transmissions, and learn what you can.

Anything you can learn about working with tools will help you understand the jobs in this category. Power saws, cranes, boats and motors, cement work, electronic gear (including ham radios), tractors—the more familiar you are with these tools and skills, the better feeling you will have for this kind of work.

Scientific, laboratory jobs

People with scientific interests are in these jobs. To learn more about them, try to get some experience working in a laboratory, even if it's only washing test tubes. Or learn to program a computer through your school, then find an after-school job in an office, doing data processing tasks. Try your local university, or some industrial firm. If you can't find a job, volunteer to work with a local environmental project so you can learn something about scientific procedures. Many hobbies require some chemical or biological procedures; learn what you can. It will help you decide later if you want to become a technician or scientist.

Artistic, musical, literary jobs

People with artistic interests work in many places besides art studios. They are interior decorators, photographers, music teachers, writers, actors, and actresses. You can gain some relevant experiences here by working in art galleries or museums, in furniture or paint stores, in advertising offices or photography studios, or in theaters. Handling assignments on school newspapers, or painting stage sets, or helping with the redecorating of your own home are other ways to gain some experiences in these areas.

Social, working-with-others jobs

Jobs such as social worker, school counselor, and YMCA/YWCA staff member are filled with people who like to work closely with others. You can easily gain experience in such areas by working in a social agency as a volunteer. You can work with young people or elderly people, or in hospitals, or with the handicapped. Every community needs many volunteers to help in such activities, and you can contribute a great deal to others while you see if you enjoy working in such settings.

Enterprising, sales, persuasive jobs

In these jobs, people are generally trying to persuade other people to do or buy something. The jobs range widely from politics to public relations, from sales to fund-raising campaigns. You can gain experience in these activities by taking part in political campaigns, by being active in student government, by working as a sales clerk, or by selling things door-to-door. If you like trying to persuade other people to your viewpoint, then you might enjoy these activities. (In addition, you might have an impact on your local politics, or as a salesperson, you might make some pocket money.)

Conventional, methodical, office jobs

In the sixth category are mainly office jobs. To gain some experience here, you need to work in an office. Even if you have the lowliest job, you can still gain useful experience about what this kind of work is like, and you can gain some skills such as typing, filing, or running a duplicating machine that can help you later no matter what career you select.

Wise men and women have written for centuries about the value of experience, and the futility of learning in any other way. James Lowell, the poet, said, "One thorn of experience is worth a whole wilderness of warning."

In planning your career, nothing will substitute for experience in helping you find your eventual niche, and *you will have to spend several years gaining that experience.* Count on it, prepare for it, and take maximum advantage of it, and if you occasionally goof up, take consolation in a comment by Bill Vaughan, a sportswriter for the *Kansas City Star:* "In the game of life, it's a good idea to have a few early losses; it relieves the pressure of trying to maintain an undefeated season."

"One thorn of experience
is worth a whole wilderness
of warning."

VIII Your Appearance

Like it or not, your looks are going to have some impact on your career. Psychological research has firmly established that our reaction to people is affected somewhat by their appearance; we tend to think more positively of attractive people, which means that attractive people have more options available to them than do unattractive ones. In commenting about the restricted opportunities available to the latter, a newspaper columnist once put it cryptically, "Her face was her chaperone." This may not seem fair—you may think that people should respond to what the other person is really like inside. After all, beauty is only skin deep, right? True, but for many purposes skin deep is deep enough.

Consequently, attractive people have a slight edge on the rest of us; the edge is only slight, but it occasionally makes a difference, and in some occupations—fashion modeling, for example—the edge is all that matters.

Well, you say, looks may be important, but I can't do anything about mine, so what's the difference? Not completely true. You can take what you have and make the best of it. You can, for example, control your own weight; many people sacrifice a considerable amount of their natural attractiveness by being plump. Stay slender, you'll look better. Pay attention to how you dress and groom yourself. You needn't always look like you're going to the Palace Ball, but you shouldn't look like you just crawled out of the dungeon, either.

One specific reason that you should look your best is that it gives a substantial boost to your self-esteem. We all have a large slice of vanity, and few things make us feel more self-confident than the feeling we are looking our best.

There are many sources of advice about appearance—books, magazines, newspapers, etc.—and you should take note of them. Do what you can with what you have; the better you handle it, the more you will have going for you.

Looks aren't everything, of course. This chapter is devoted to many assets, and your appearance is only one. The point is: Take advantage of it where you can; cut your losses where you can't.

Let me mention one other point that may make you feel better. Several years ago, when I was a professor of psychology at the University of Minnesota, I did a study of some of the world's most beautiful women, fashion models from New York and Paris. One thing I learned from that research is that it is possible to be too beautiful, both because beautiful people develop exaggerated opinions of their own value and because it turns their heads from developing other assets. Many of these young women made enormous sums of money simply for standing still and having their pictures taken. Although they were handsomely rewarded and their egos were momentarily fed by seeing their pictures on the covers of millions of magazines, the experience didn't teach them how to do anything else. When their beauty faded, as it always did, many of them had nothing else to fall back on. They had depended on their appearance to open doors, to give them employment, to give them a sense of personal value; when their beauty went, everything else went with it.

Of course, some of these women were planful; they developed other skills such as acting, or merchandising, or even occasionally politics. Their beauty, along with a specific skill, gave them a head start, and the combination was effective. Beautiful women, and men, too, who are also talented, will find many future pathways open to them.

That is the whole purpose of this book; to show you how to combine your assets to become a more effective person, and to help you avoid the pitfall of running out of assets.

IX Your Health

Good health is your most important asset; without it, your other assets become almost irrelevant. The Chinese say it well: "Fame, fortune, family, and friends can all be represented by zeros. Health can be represented by the number '1.' If you have the '1' to put first, every added zero increases your wealth. Without the '1,' you have nothing."

Fortunately, in our society good medical advice is generally available. Most people have a family doctor or clinic. In addition, doctors and health scientists write columns for newspapers and magazines, and many institutions have public health services such as nurses in schools or medical offices in industrial plants. Good information is available if you will pay attention to it.

Three potential medical problems are so widespread in America that you need to pay special attention to them in planning your life. Hopefully, with prior planning, you can avoid these three health problems that plague so many people: (1) overweight, (2) lack of exercise, and (3) drug dependency (mainly tobacco and alcohol).

1 *Overweight.* Experts say that at least one-third of the people in America are overweight; a day at the beach is enough to convince me that that is probably an underestimate. Being overweight has several disadvantages, the first one being that fat people die younger, and in planning a successful career, death is a definite handicap. Further, while alive, fat people do not advance as far in the world as slender ones. One research project showed, for example, that salaries of fat people are lower than those of thin people with the same training and experience. Another study showed that obese girls are more often rejected by colleges than are normal-weight girls with the same high school grades and test scores.

How do you avoid being overweight? Two main ways are watching your eating habits and exercising. Many books have been written on the subject of diets; one of them, for example, is Jean Mayer's book, *Overweight: Causes, Cost, and Control.* Get one of them and educate yourself about diets and eating.

Recognize one crucial point: The eating habits you grow up with are going to follow you the rest of your life, so you should begin early to develop the proper habits.

2 *Exercise.* Even if you eat well and keep your weight down, you can abuse your body by not staying active. Again, early habits are crucial here. Unless you take up some energetic activities early in life and maintain them into adulthood, you are likely to lapse into a sedentary life that includes too much television and not enough sweat. Learn to do something *every day.* Walk briskly at least, or jog, or swim, or play tennis, or bicycle, or play handball. Do calisthenics, too, if you can, but my impression is that few people have the self-discipline to stay with calisthenics.

Friends are important here also. Pick yourself some active ones. If your friends care about staying in shape, so will you. If they are active, you are more likely to be. If they play handball or tennis, or ride bicycles, you are more likely to do so with them. If you socialize with overweight friends, you will find yourself carrying around their weight also. You will go to too many cocktail parties, drink too much beer, eat too much rich food. Overweight people usually eat and drink a lot, and you will be doing the same. If you want to watch your own waistline, watch those of your friends.

3 *Drugs.* Roughly one person in three in America smokes, despite overwhelming evidence that smoking leads to a variety of diseases such as lung cancer, heart attacks, and emphysema. Many smokers want to stop but they are hooked, even though they know they are ruining their bodies and shortening their lives. Take a lesson from them; it is much easier never to start than to break what many people find to be an unbreakable habit.

Alcohol is another drug that leads to serious medical problems. A drink now and then— even an occasional blast—does little harm, but several million people have escalated from "a drink now and then" into alcoholism. Again, it is largely a matter of the wrong habits learned early. If you are aware of the problem and are determined to be cautious, you will likely not have any trouble.

There are various other drugs that get people into trouble: marijuana, barbiturates, heroin, etc. Most people have already made up their minds about whether or not these drugs are dangerous, and when arguments are made to try to change their minds, they resist. If you think marijuana is a dangerous drug, you are obviously going to be careful about using it. If you think it is harmless, then any cautions that I might raise will probably not convince you. I won't try, other than to say that there are considerable data available about the effects of such drugs on your body. The data are conflicting and confusing, and all experts don't agree. Yet, in my personal opinion, there are enough disturbing reports to give me pause. If there is a possibility of long-term physical damage to your body, is the momentary thrill worth it?

Your Assets: A Summing Up

In this chapter I have outlined some of the main factors that will influence your future choices. No one has all of these assets going for them; no one has none of them. As always, most of us fall somewhere in the middle, but with planning and effort we can improve our standing, and thus our breadth of choice.

So, work on your assets to increase your options, and never lose track of the point made in the first chapter, that no matter how well life goes for you, you will never "arrive," you will only be always on the way.

Unless you take up
some energetic activities
early in life
and maintain them . . .

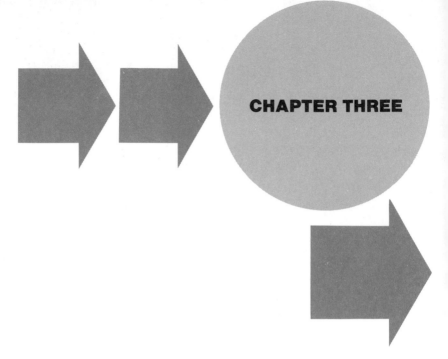

CHAPTER THREE

The law of work does seem utterly unfair—but there it is, and nothing can change it; the higher the pay in enjoyment the worker gets out of it, the higher shall be his pay in money also.

Mark Twain

If You Want Something to Happen, Make a Space for It

The most important influence on your life-style is going to be your occupation. It will determine not only what you do every day, but it will also greatly affect how you live, who your friends are, what clothes you wear, when you take vacations, how much money you make, and how long you have to work.

Most important, your work will have an enormous impact on how you think about yourself, because we identify more closely with our occupations than with anything else. When people ask, "What are you going to be when you grow up?" everyone answers with a job: "I'm going to be a teacher, or a politician, or an interior decorator, or a dentist." No one ever says, "I'm going to be a Southerner, or a happy person, or a Republican." Although many people will be Southerners, and happy people, and Republicans, no one ever uses those terms to define his or her own future.

The same is true of adults. Ask the nearest person, "Who are you?" and the response will be something like, "I am a cab driver, or a beautician, or a lawyer, or a farmer." No one ever says, "I am a five-foot, eight-inch, 150-pound parent of three children." No one ever says, "I am a lover," or "I am an extrovert," or "I am a U.S. citizen." Our self-images are dominated by our occupations.

Because your job is so important in determining your life-style and your self-image, you had better give that aspect of your future a great deal of attention. Your job will define you, so you had better study the different kinds of jobs pretty closely.

There are six basic categories of occupations, and every job can be grouped into one of these categories or some combination of them. In outline form, here are the categories as they were developed by Professor John L. Holland, a psychology professor from Johns Hopkins University, who has studied occupations for years:

Realistic. These are mainly skilled trades or technical jobs, usually involving work with tools or machines, frequently called "blue-collar" positions.

Investigative. These are scientific and laboratory jobs, jobs where people investigate how the world is put together.

Artistic. These are creative jobs where people work with words, or music, or art.

Social. These are jobs where people work with people—healing them, teaching them, helping them.

Enterprising. These are jobs where people persuade other people to do something—sales jobs, political jobs, merchandising jobs.

Conventional. These are usually office jobs where people work with organizations, files, and regular schedules.

These categories can be thought of as a circle or hexagon, with the categories most alike being located next to each other.

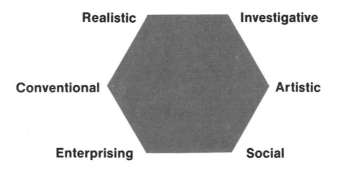

The categories most similar to each other are nearest to each other; those most dissimilar are farthest away, opposite each other across the diagonal.

Some jobs fall directly into one category—"auto mechanic," for example, falls directly into the *realistic* category, and "secretary" falls directly into the *conventional* category. Other jobs fall somewhere in between—"art teacher," for example, falls about halfway between *artistic* and *social,* and "sales manager" falls about halfway between *enterprising* and *conventional.*

In planning your career, you should concentrate on that portion of the hexagon that attracts you the most, and to do that you need to know more about the jobs around the hexagon and more about yourself.

Jobs differ in three important ways:

1 The actual work involved on the job.
2 The type of coworkers attracted to each job.
3 The unique rewards of each kind of job.

The first difference is *the work itself,* what you actually do all day—whether you build things, or sell things, or create new things; whether you work with tools, or with ideas, or with people; whether you do this outside, or in an office, or in a factory.

The second difference between types of jobs is *the people you work with,* and their most important characteristic is what they like to do. If you work in a laboratory, you are going to be working around people who like to work with lab equipment; if you work in an art museum, you are going to be working around people who like art; if you work in a school, you are going to be working around people who like students; if you work on a construction crew, you are going to be working around people who like to work with tools and machines. These differences in the interests of your coworkers will create very different work environments.

The third important difference between jobs is *the kind of rewards* that you receive from your work. By rewards, I don't mean money, but rather the kind of feelings you will gain from doing a good job. For example, in the *artistic* jobs, you will have many opportunities to create things, and your satisfactions will come from the thrill of creativity. In the *social* jobs, you will have many opportunities to help people. If you do that well, your reward will be the satisfying glow that comes from helping other people. In the *conventional* jobs, you will have an opportunity to help an organization function smoothly. If you do that well, your reward will be the satisfaction of seeing programs run smoothly and the institution function effectively.

The six types of jobs are described here in some detail. Recognize that I am describing extremes; no one job fits all of these comments exactly. When I talk about the characteristics of people in the jobs, recognize that no one person has all of these characteristics. I am talking about trends, but they are strong trends.

Realistic

Tasks

Some typical *realistic* tasks:

1 Run a large bulldozer.
2 Build a chest out of wood.
3 Operate an X-ray machine.
4 Take apart a small engine.
5 Wire a summer cabin.

The tasks involved in *realistic* jobs usually involve working with tools or machines and sometimes working outdoors or on construction sites. The tools might be large, powerful machines such as bulldozers, cranes, tractors, or big trucks, or the tools might be precision machinery such as X-ray machines or watchmaker's tools. People in *realistic* jobs might work with wrenches, hammers, surveying equipment, electrical equipment, or construction machinery. The jobs might involve working on cars, boats, airplanes, pumps, or automatic, high-speed packaging machinery. *Realistic* jobs frequently involve either building something new such as houses, machinery, roads, and bridges, or maintaining such structures after they are completed.

Coworkers

People who are attracted to *realistic* jobs are usually rugged, robust, practical, physically strong, and frequently competitive in outlook. They usually have good physical coordination, but sometimes they have trouble expressing themselves in words or in talking with others. They like to work outdoors, and they like to work with tools, especially large, powerful machines. They prefer to deal with things rather than with ideas or with people. They generally have conventional political and economic opinions, and they are usually cool to radical new ideas. They enjoy creating things with their hands. They have good motor coordination, but they are frequently uncomfortable in social settings, and lack verbal and interpersonal skills. They usually see themselves as mechanically and athletically inclined and are stable, natural, and persistent. They prefer concrete to abstract problems. They rarely perform creatively in the arts or the sciences, but they do enjoy building things. *Realistic* people tend to see the world in simple, tangible, and traditional terms. Possessions are important to them, and they usually put their recreational money into cars, boats, campers, snowmobiles, motorcycles, airplanes, or other machinery.

Realistic people describe themselves in interviews as "conforming, frank, genuine, normal, persistent, practical, stable, thrifty, materialistic, shy, and uninvolved."

Rewards

One unique reward of most *realistic* jobs is that life appears relatively simple and straightforward, and the worker can quickly see the results of his or her labors. The mechanic who is working on a car can see at the end of the job that the car now functions. The carpenter building a house has the quiet satisfaction of seeing the house take shape. The forester harvesting logs can watch the pile of logs grow and can quickly see the fruits of a day's labor. The person who is working on a machine such as a drill press can see the material being formed. The machine adjuster working on a high-speed packing line can quickly see the speed with which materials are being produced. In general, on *realistic* jobs, life is not complicated by intricate problems between people or organizations, nor by troublesome choices between conflicting philosophies.

Investigative

Tasks

Some typical *investigative* tasks:

1 Read scientific reports.
2 Work on new, exotic computer applications.
3 Study blood samples through a microscope.
4 Build laboratory equipment.
5 Look through scientific data for basic trends.

The tasks involved in *investigative* jobs are scientific or laboratory in nature, and usually involve trying to solve some puzzle, whether the puzzle is a large, mysterious problem such as how the universe came into being, or a more normal, daily problem such as figuring out the composition of a sample of blood taken from a patient in a medical clinic. *Investigative* or scientific jobs usually involve working in laboratories, clinics, or other research settings. The work usually involves charts and graphs, numbers and formulas, and data about a wide variety of physical phenomena such as the load-bearing characteristics of materials, or the composition of the voting records of an entire state, or the protein composition of different foods. Frequently, these tasks require long periods of intellectual effort, and people have been known to spend all night or entire weekends working on scientific problems.

Investigative workers are usually found in research laboratories or clinical settings, but they also work in a wide range of other places—highway departments where they study issues such as traffic control and composition of highway materials; in advertising agencies where they work on market surveys; in food producing companies where they work on nutritional aspects of food; in military settings where they work on new weapons or new military strategies; in financial departments where they work on questions of economic strategy, money flow, and inventory problems—in general, in any place where problems are being attacked in a systematic, scientific way.

Investigative tasks frequently involve the use of computers, microscopes, telescopes, volt meters, high-speed centrifuges, or any of an incredible array of other laboratory and scientific equipment. The *investigative* job differs from the *realistic* job in that the *realistic* job is usually more concerned with machines that produce products, while the *investigative* job is concerned with machines that produce data or information.

Coworkers

People in *investigative* jobs are task-oriented, which means they get all wrapped up in the problem they are working on. For the most part they are not particularly interested in working around other people. They prefer to work independently, and they usually don't like to be supervised or to supervise other people. They sometimes perceive themselves as lacking in leadership or persuasive abilities, but they are confident of their scholarly and intellectual abilities.

They enjoy solving abstract problems and have a great need to understand the physical world; this includes a reverence for "hard data" and a reluctance to accept unquestioningly "traditional wisdom."

They prefer to think through problems rather than act them out. They enjoy ambiguous challenges and do not like highly structured situations with lots of rules. They frequently have unconventional values and attitudes and tend to be original and creative, especially in scientific areas. They are frequently asocial and do not enjoy large social gatherings.

They describe themselves as "analytical, curious, independent, and reserved." They especially dislike repetitive activities and sales activities. They are very curious.

Rewards

The unique reward of many *investigative* jobs is the worker's freedom and opportunity to satisfy an innate curiosity. Scientists are continually curious about nature, about people, about business, even about art and music, and are continually studying all of these areas, using a scientific approach—analyzing situations, checking out data, trying to understand what is going on in whatever field they are working.

In addition, *investigative* jobs usually allow the worker considerable freedom to try out new ways. People are allowed to indulge their own work-styles, though of course there is steady pressure for achievement.

Artistic

Tasks

Some typical *artistic* tasks:

1 Paint someone's portrait.
2 Act in a play.
3 Take music lessons.
4 Read or write poetry.
5 Design a new type of fabric.

The tasks involved in *artistic* occupations usually involve the creation of artistic products, working with words, music, or other art forms. Some other examples of specific activities are painting or sketching pictures, composing or playing music, writing or performing plays, playing in an orchestra or band. Decorating rooms, designing homes, or doing portrait photography are other examples of artistic activities.

Artistic jobs are found in settings such as art museums, art galleries, music departments, interior decorating offices, music stores, theater groups, photographic studios, radio and television stations, and any place where artistic skills are taught—music departments, art departments, theater departments, and, to a lesser extent, departments of journalism or schools of architecture.

Coworkers

People who enjoy working in *artistic* jobs describe themselves as "complicated, disorderly, emotional, idealistic, imaginative, impractical, impulsive, independent, introspective, intuitive, nonconforming, and original." They like to work in free environments that allow them to express themselves in a wide variety of media—writing, music, drawing, acting, photography, fabrics—in general, any art form or material.

They value beauty and esthetic qualities, and don't care much for social entanglements.

They like small, intimate groups and generally don't like large "country-club type" affairs. They like to make things, especially new and different things, and are willing to take risks to try something new even if the chances of failure are high.

Many artistic people feel driven to produce their own distinct product; they try to express their personalities in their output, and they feel very uncomfortable in settings where they have to inhibit themselves. Artistic people usually dress in freer styles than other people; if everyone else is wearing suits, they prefer jeans. If everyone else is wearing jeans, they prefer capes, or caftans, or muumuus— something distinctive, something that expresses their individuality. Artistic people have a distaste for appearing conventional or undistinguished. They like to use their creativity to help them stand out from the crowd.

Artistic people have little interest in problems that are highly structured or that require a lot of physical strength, preferring those problems that can be dealt with by means of self-expression and artistic media. They resemble *investigative* people in preferring to work alone, but have a greater need for individualistic expression, are usually less assertive about their own capabilities, and are more sensitive and emotional. *Artistic* people score higher on measures of creativity than any of the other types. Other adjectives they use to describe themselves are "independent, original, unconventional, expressive, and intense."

Rewards

The unique reward of *artistic* jobs comes from the opportunities for creating new things, and from being around other creative people. In most creative jobs the person is expected every day to create something new, to try something different, to stretch for new ways. This continual stimulation for the new and the different, for quality in creativity, is a primary reward of artistic jobs. Creative coworkers create an atmosphere in which this continual striving for innovation is tolerated, even encouraged.

Social

Tasks

Some typical *social* tasks:

1 Teach someone how to read.
2 Help a friend patch up a broken romance.
3 Organize a round-table discussion about different religions.
4 Work with an adoption agency.
5 Write letters for someone in the hospital.

The tasks involved in *social* jobs are those concerned with working with other people, teaching them, or training them, or curing them, or leading them, or organizing them, or enlightening them. Examples of *social* jobs are high school teacher, speech therapist, physical education teacher, playground director, clinical psychologist, vocational counselor, or city school superintendent. *Social* tasks include explaining things to others, entertaining other people, planning the teaching of other people, helping other people solve their difficulties, organizing and conducting charities, and straightening out differences between people.

Coworkers

People who enjoy working in *social* jobs describe themselves as "cooperative, friendly, generous, helptul, idealistic, responsible, sociable, tactful, and understanding." They like to work in groups, especially small groups that are working on problems common to individuals in the group.

They dislike working with machines or in highly organized situations such as military units. They like to discuss philosophic questions—the purpose of life, what constitutes right or wrong. They are socially competent and like situations that allow them to display their social values, such as leading group discussions.

Social people are concerned with the welfare of others. They usually express themselves well and get along well with others. They like attention and seek situations that allow them to be at or near the center of the group. They prefer to solve problems by discussions with others, or by arranging or rearranging relationships between others. Social people also describe themselves as "cheerful, popular, achieving, and good leaders.

Rewards

The rewards of working in *social* jobs center around the warm glow that comes from helping other people solve their problems or improve themselves. People from all walks of life are called on occasionally to help their friends in time of trouble, but people in *social* jobs are called upon daily for that kind of help; indeed, they are usually paid to give it—it's their job. Consequently, they often have opportunities to work closely with other people and help them out, and they have frequent opportunities to see the results of how their actions helped others. People in *social* jobs usually have coworkers who are like themselves, and groups of social people are usually warm and supportive of each other. They make each other feel wanted, they have great respect for each other's abilities, and they have many opportunities for close interpersonal relationships.

Enterprising
Tasks

Some typical *enterprising* tasks:

1 Lead an important committee.
2 Give a speech on your organization's policies.

3 Run for an elected office.
4 Head up a fund-raising campaign.
5 Take a course in leadership development.

Enterprising jobs involve persuading other people to your viewpoint. Included are many sales jobs, political jobs, leadership jobs, and business executive jobs. Some examples of the daily activities of *enterprising* people are selling things to other people, running meetings where groups are trying to set standards or arrive at goals, handling situations where new policies or procedures are being debated. *Enterprising* activities involve organizing committees, running task forces, planning new organizational structures, worrying about how to motivate others, and trying to plan relationships between people so that the group will be effective. Examples of *enterprising* jobs include business executives, salespeople, political campaign managers, public relations directors, stock and bond brokers, buyers, retailers, fashion merchandisers, and industrial consultants.

Coworkers

People who enjoy working in *enterprising* jobs describe themselves as "adventuresome, ambitious, argumentative, domineering, energetic, flirtatious, impulsive, optimistic, self-confident, sociable, and talkative."

Such people enjoy competitive activities and like to work in groups where they can have some influence over what the group is doing. They are self-confident and usually see themselves as good leaders. Usually they are fairly good speakers, both in groups and in one-to-one conversations. They are persuasive, and they enjoy trying to make things happen.

Enterprising people value money and material possessions; frequently, they drive expensive cars and have expensive hobbies such as sailing large boats or flying their own airplanes. Many *enterprising* people like to belong to country clubs and the best social groups; they enjoy trips to resort hotels, and they like to meet and hobnob with famous, rich, and powerful people. Generally, *enterprising* people dislike science and systematic thinking.

Enterprising people usually have a great facility with words, which they put to effective use in selling, dominating, and leading. They are impatient with detail work or work involving long periods of heavy thinking. They like power, status, and material wealth; they enjoy working in expensive settings. They have strong drives to organizational goals or economic aims. They see themselves as aggressive, popular, self-confident, cheerful, and sociable. They generally have a high energy level and lots of enthusiasm.

Rewards

The unique reward from *enterprising* jobs is the sense of achievement that comes from making things happen, whether it is conducting a sales campaign, or winning an election, or persuading a board of directors to accept new policies. *Enterprising* people frequently have a strong sense of relevance from being where the action is.

Conventional

Tasks

Some typical *conventional* tasks:

1 Preparing written reports.
2 Keeping careful records.
3 Typing and filing reports and correspondence.
4 Organizing office procedures.
5 Operating business machines.

Conventional occupations include bookkeeper, statistician, bank teller, inventory controller, payroll clerk, secretary, financial analyst, office manager, computer operator, bank cashier, and accountant. *Conventional* jobs usually require a fair amount of writing, but it is usually the writing of business letters and regular reports rather than the writing of poetry, plays, or short stories.

Coworkers

People who enjoy *conventional* jobs describe themselves as "conforming, conscientious, efficient, inhibited, obedient, orderly, persistent, practical, and calm."

They like for life to be orderly and to go according to plan. They like to know what is expected of them, and they enjoy carrying out their assignments. They prefer regular hours for work and like to work in comfortable, indoor environments. Usually, they are averse to free, unsystematic exploratory behavior in new areas.

Conventional people prefer the highly ordered activities, both verbal and numerical, that characterize office work. They fit well into large organizations but do not themselves seek out leadership; consequently, they prefer to work within a well-established chain of command. They dislike ambiguity and prefer to know precisely what is expected of them. They describe themselves as "conventional, stable, well-controlled, and dependable." They have little interest in problems requiring physical skills or intense relationships with others, and they are most effective at well-defined tasks. Like enterprising people, they value material possessions and status, although they usually prefer conforming and subordinate roles.

Rewards

The rewards of working in *conventional* jobs center around seeing offices and organizations run smoothly, and in understanding how the individual's contribution helps in making that happen. People who have a methodical outlook on life, who can organize, and who can keep a million details straight so that the work of other people is facilitated take great pleasure in seeing their efforts result in a smooth-running operation. People in *conventional* positions are frequently the glue that holds the entire operation together. Because of the nature of their work, they are not always publicly recognized as much as perhaps they should be, but they themselves have some appreciation of the contribution they are making to the organization, and this is one of the pleasant aspects of *conventional* occupations.

Now that you have some notion as to the various types of jobs and their characteristics, let's review the structure of the world of work, using some examples. Pages 124–25 show the hexagon again, this time with several jobs written in to illustrate the types. Remember, these are only averages; people in each of these occupations are not all alike. This classification system is not perfect, but the trends are clear.

Use this illustration as a guide to help you learn more about occupations. Focus on that part of the hexagon that appeals most to you, then set out to learn more about the occupations in that part of the structure.

How do you learn which part of the hexagon appeals to you most? Well, that takes a little effort. First, look at the typical tasks listed for each type and decide which cluster appeals most to you. Maybe more than one cluster

RI
Auto mechanic
Machinist
Military officer

R
Carpenter
Civil engineer
Electrician

RC
Draftsman
Farmer
Police officer

Realistic

CR
Dental assistant
Sewing machine operator
Telephone operator

C
Accountant
Computer operator
Secretary

Conventional

CE
Banker
Business education teacher
Office worker

EC
Corporation executive
Manufacturer
Stockbroker

Enterprising

E
Lawyer
Politician
Retailer

ES
Chamber of Commerce director
Life insurance sales
Public relations director

IR
Electrical engineer
Inventor
Lab technician

I
Biologist
Scientific researcher
Technical writer

Investigative

IA
Astronomer
College professor
Economist

AI
Psychologist
Photographer
Sculptor

A
Artist
Librarian
Musician

Artistic

AS
Dancing teacher
English teacher
Drama coach

SA
Music teacher
Author, children's books
Home economist

Social

S
Social worker
Church worker
Public health nurse

SE
School principal
YMCA/YWCA staff
Labor arbitrator

attracts you; then you should look at occupations that fall between the clusters.

Second, if this approach still doesn't help you, then seek out your counselor and ask for guidance. Ask to take a vocational interest inventory; these are professionally developed questionnaires that will help you understand yourself in relation to the world of work. One of the more widely used inventories is the *Strong-Campbell Interest Inventory;* your scores on this inventory will show how you compare, in your interests, with employed people in a wide range of occupations and will help you understand how your interests fit into the occupational world. (If your counselor is unfamiliar with this inventory, more information can be secured from its publisher, Stanford University Press, Stanford, California.) Filling in an inventory such as this one and then discussing the results with a professionally trained counselor will provide you with a more substantial base for career planning than you might achieve on your own. Don't be reluctant to seek advice from people who know more and who have had more experience than you have had.

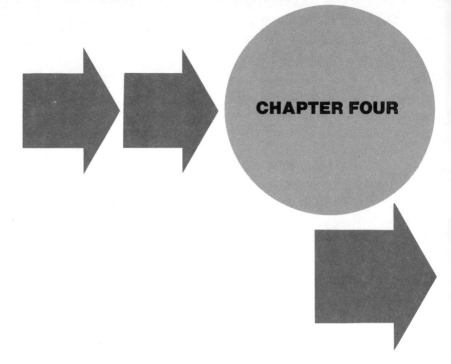

CHAPTER FOUR

Sophie Tucker, when asked on her
eightieth birthday about the secret
of achieving a long life, answered:
"Keep breathing."

Live, Love, and Laugh

A few main themes have continually run through the earlier chapters of this book; let me summarize them here.

First, you need to have some goals—"if you don't know where you're going, you will probably wind up somewhere else."

Second, selecting your goals is a matter of choosing which direction you want to go, not choosing specific places at which you want to end up. Life is in the running, not in the arriving.

Third, the possible directions that you can take will depend almost entirely on the number of assets you have going for you. Consequently, to expand your choices you should be continually cultivating your assets. *You* will have to take the initiative. As the fellow said, "People who want milk should not seat themselves on a stool in the middle of a field in hopes that the cow will back up to them."

. . . your career
is going to determine
how you live.

Fourth, with few exceptions your achievements will be won gradually, not overnight, and you should proceed accordingly. The Persians had a proverb: "Do little things now; so shall big things come to thee by and by asking to be done."

Fifth, more than any other factor, your job—or more generally, your career—is going to determine how you live. Thus, give it a great deal of attention and thought. Those in this world who do not work, either by choice or by circumstance, do not amount to much. Usually, they don't even like themselves.

Sixth, basic to everything is health. Take care of your body; it is your instrument of life. With health, you have a chance; without it, nothing.

Finally, have fun. Don't take yourself too seriously. One of your first goals should be to develop a healthy perspective. Laugh a lot. Tear out the last page of this book and tape it to the ceiling above your bed where you will see it every morning.

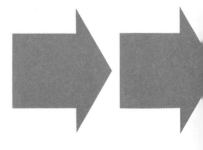

There's more

. . . have fun.
Don't take yourself too seriously. . . .
Laugh a lot.

. . . and there's still more

HA HA HO HO HEE HEE

**Be glad of life
because it gives
you the chance
to love and to work
and to play and to
look at the stars.**

Henry van Dyke